DINOSAURS,

THE LOST WORLD, AND YOU

John D. Morris

Master Books

First printing: May 1999
Second printing: September 2001

ISBN: 0-89051-256-6
Library of Congress Number: 99-70692

Cover by Janell Robertson
Cover illustrations by Lloyd R. Hight

Previously published by Institute for Creation Research.

Printed in the United States of America.

Please visit our website for other great titles:
www.masterbooks.net

For information regarding publicity for author interviews contact Dianna Fletcher at (870) 438-5288.

Author's Note

"Millions of years ago, when dinosaurs ruled the earth, long before man evolved . . ." so begin many children's books about dinosaurs. In adult books and movies, the message remains the same. Any new dinosaur discovery is always big news. Everyone, young and old, is fascinated by dinosaurs — those huge, ugly monsters, which the entertainment industry portrays as fearsome hunters!

Summer 1993 brought several dinosaur movies to theaters. The box office hit *Jurassic Park* featured live dinosaurs recreated through cloning, accomplished by extracting DNA from dinosaur blood preserved in the amber-encased bodies of mosquitoes dead for millions of years. Of course, the movie plot included the dinosaurs breaking loose and wreaking havoc, much to the thrill of movie-goers.

During the spring of 1997, *The Lost World*, the sequel to *Jurassic Park*, was released. Both of these movies were based on science fiction novels written by Michael Crichton. Throughout the movies and books, information about dinosaur evolution is subtly and not so subtly conveyed. These films also popularized the "chaos theory," which is incorrectly used to promote many evolutionary ideas. Crichton researched and interviewed many prominent evolutionary scientists and researchers as background for his works. Much of the information (not the plot) on dinosaurs reflects the views of the well-known dinosaur paleontologist, Jack Horner, but some of his rather unique views are controversial, even among other paleontologists and evolutionary scientists. Crichton's works feature some highly intelligent dinosaurs that stalk humans and exhibit other debatable behaviors and characteristics: some dinosaurs live in herds, others hunt in packs, still others spit poison, and parent dinosaurs care for their offspring after hatching. Obviously, these abilities and behavior patterns are not proven scientific fact; they may be entirely wrong.

The wide interest in dinosaurs — and the vast misinformation regarding them — accentuates the need for this booklet, which intends to answer some common questions and give a sound biblical understanding of these fascinating and wonderful creatures. Today, such an understanding becomes vital, as dinosaurs are now being used to promote the anti-Christian world view of evolutionary pantheism.

Perhaps more importantly, we will learn that scientists have biases too, and at times these biases interfere with an honest evaluation of the evidence. The creation interpretation presented here may be new for some readers, but I believe it more closely adheres to the facts and better explains the scientific evidence.

I. EVOLUTION OR CREATION?

Many of my scientific colleagues reconstruct the past and interpret the fossil evidence to support the evolutionary view. They feel that some three or four billion years ago, non-living chemicals sprang to life as a single-celled organism. Eventually, this "simple" life evolved into multicellular life, producing a vast array of marine invertebrates some six hundred million years ago. "Soon" fish, amphibians, and reptiles evolved into existence. Dinosaurs supposedly ruled the earth approximately 220 million years ago until they all became extinct some 65 million years ago. All this occurred, according to evolution, through strictly *natural* processes, operating totally at random, with no directing mind guiding life's development.

Obviously, fossils don't come with labels on them, explaining what each creature was like, where it came from, and when and how it lived. Fossils from the past must be interpreted. History is reconstructed according to an individual's *belief* of the past, but this belief can never be proven; it is held for *philosophical* reasons. Highly qualified scientists often work from a bias based on philosophy; therefore, evolution is best understood as philosophy, not science.

Evolutionary thinking dominates the schools, the media, and the entertainment industry. However, there are many scientists who have rejected evolution for philosophical *and* scientific reasons. Evolution has never been well supported by the fossil evidence, and much of the available evidence doesn't conform to evolutionary theory at all. Life, from the simplest single-celled organism, to the largest dinosaur, to the human body, exhibits a majestic design that appears to be in direct opposition to random evolutionary change.

Macroevolution Versus Microevolution

Often textbooks and newspapers cloud the truth by confusing terms. While sometimes referred to simply as "change," evolution, at least in the meaningful sense, implies *enormous* changes in organisms. People supposedly came from ape-like ancestors, which came from a rat-like animal, which came from a fish, which came from an animal with no skeleton, which came from a single-celled organism. The proper term for this large-scale change is *macro*evolution. This macroevolution has never been proven, for it has never been observed.

Frequently, what is observed scientifically is *micro*evolution. Microevolution refers to small changes within an animal type. No new features are produced, but varying traits are expressed. This is also called adaptation or variation. *All* the proposed examples of observed change are *micro*evolutionary changes.

Scientifically proven examples of microevolution are: certain microbes' acquired resistance to antibiotics, pesticide-resistant insects, a color pattern shift in the peppered moth in England, and taller people today than those who lived long ago. Do these changes tell us anything about how people evolved from fish? Obviously not!

Creationists agree with small, microevolutionary changes. The question is, does microevolution lead to macroevolution? There is no evidence that it does now, or that it has ever done so in the past.

One possible source of significant change is that of mutations — the sudden, random, altering of a particular gene, which could then be passed on to offspring. Again, true science must ask, "What has been observed?" Although thousands of mutations have been observed, and thousands more have been induced, never once has a mutation benefited an organism or produced any *new* trait or functioning organ. No mutation which could contribute to macroevolution is known to science. Most mutations are neutral, many are harmful, and some are fatal. Therefore, it appears that random change in the genetic code cannot improve it.

The most common claim of a beneficial mutation is the fatal disease sickle-cell anemia. Carriers do have a better chance of not contracting malaria, but the consequences of sickle-cell anemia are far more detrimental and may even result in death. We can conclude, then, that macroevolutionary ideas are not supported by scientific observation.

The Second Law of Thermodynamics

The observed laws of science provide a huge barrier to evolution. A basic law of science, known as the "second law of thermodynamics," has been observed and verified in every field of science. This law reveals a general trend toward deterioration in all of nature. Everything moves in a downward spiral toward a less ordered state. Stars burn out. The moon's orbit is decaying. Cars wear out. Wood rots. Living plants wither and fade. Animals die. People get sick and grow old. No exception to this rule of decline has ever been observed.

Let's relate this to evolution. The genetic code is unimaginably complex, and this code specifies everything about life, from conception to growth. Scientists have only begun to understand the work DNA performs. Partial functions of some genes have been identified, but no gene has been fully decoded. Usually genes perform several functions and several genes work together to do each job. Is it credible to claim that a *random* change in this highly complex system could increase its complexity and improve its function? Could a mutation in a gene produce a new body part, or even a slight improvement in a part's ability in spite of the dominant trend of the second law of thermodynamics?

Creationists have long emphasized the anti-evolutionary implications of this law of science. Evolutionists have responded by appealing to an abundance of energy in the environment, claiming that there is plenty of energy available to produce any change needed. An example given for this increased order is a seed growing into a plant, utilizing the sun's ample energy. However, a crucial fact is ignored — the plant *already* possesses the ability to convert the sun's energy into useful forms. This ability, photosynthesis, is already coded into the plant's genetics, which also directs the energy into the proper channels, allowing orderly growth. Growth of an existing organism says nothing of the origin of that organism, or how it would evolve into an entirely new form of life. Furthermore, the plant has not evolved into something else, and it will eventually die.

Another proposed example is that of a crystal growing out of a solution. However, this only follows well-known laws of molecular attraction and bonding and merely conforms to a repetitious pattern. There is no comparison to the much more complex patterns found in living molecules. No known law exists to order the growth of life systems. This written information is contained in the genetic code, which the rest of the cell reads, understands, and follows.

Evolution must answer this question: Where does the marvelous capacity of cells to grow and function originate? How it grows once it has this ability cannot explain this phenomenon. This basic law of science raises a considerable problem for evolution.

What about Chaos Theory?

In an attempt to remedy the failure of the traditional macroevolutionary arguments, evolutionists are considering new theories — one of which is commonly referred to as *"chaos theory."* Chaos theory, through mathematical equations, conceptual ideas, and computer simulations, seeks to model causes for ordered systems to decay into what appears to be chaos.

Used in the proper context, chaos theory is, in reality, an explanation of complex patterns in systems that previously were labeled as random, such as the weather. Weather gives the appearance of randomness that prevents meteorologists from achieving complete accuracy as they make long-term weather predictions. In actuality, weather is not random, but extremely complex. To illustrate this, consider a giant maze. While one is in the maze, attempting to find a way out, the twists and turns appear to be random. However, a view from above the maze reveals the complexity of the pattern.

Evolutionists mis-use chaos theory by claiming that the reverse is true — that it is possible for orderliness to be the result of chaotic systems, or that chaos may, given enough time, produce complexity. If this were true, then non-life would theoretically become simple life, and simple life would evolve into complex life.

Chaos theory is the result of the work of Ilya Prigogine, who authored the book *Order Out of Chaos*. Prigogine noted that energy dispersed from the heat of a cup of coffee would cause small whirlpools in the liquid. He claimed these whirlpools were ordered structures formed by raw energy in the form of heat. Prigogine also pointed out similar examples, which have become known as dissipative structures. Evolutionists hope that Prigogine's dissipative structures will eventually prove that structures can be formed by raw energy, enabling evolution to proceed toward higher levels of complexity and order. Even Prigogine himself, however, acknowledges that there is no proof that this has ever happened, or that it could happen.

In actual experiments and observation up to this point, however, the second law of thermodynamics still brands any macroevolution as impossible, in spite of the efforts of chaoticians.

As introduced earlier, evolutionists point to crystals as

another example of order from chaos. At first, it appears that the structure of crystals is much more complex than the solution from which they formed. However, the process of crystallization is in full harmony with the second law of thermodynamics. The solution itself already contains the information necessary to form the crystals. Crystal growth is specified by the laws of molecular bonding. Furthermore, the formed crystals represent a dead end. They can only disintegrate; they are not capable of forming a more ordered structure later on. The example of crystallization fails to explain how order can originate from chaos.

Finally, chaos theory considers a chaotic system as a highly complex system in which underlying order can be potentially discerned mathematically. In spite of the very technical nature of this theory, evolution of highly complex forms by the spontaneous interactions of chaos remains, at best, a theory.

What Is the "Edge of Chaos"?

The term "the edge of chaos" has been used to define the boundary between complete randomness and order. If a complex system is functioning at or near this boundary, it may collapse into total chaos, or possibly suddenly leap to a more complex state — or so the theory goes. Some evolutionists claim that this edge of chaos is where evolutionary change takes place.

Some theorize that dinosaur extinction could be explained by the edge of chaos. In this theory, the edge of chaos is the point at which a stable system becomes unstable. This edge might be the ideal place for animals to survive, balanced between stability needed to carry on life and change that allows a creature to adapt to new environments. It is a region of clash and tumult, where the old and new are in a battle. To move away from this edge of chaos would be deadly. Complete stability would mean that an animal could not adapt to changing conditions or evolve, while too much change would be just as deadly. This, according to the theory, is why dinosaurs became extinct. In theory, life thrives best at the precipitous juncture between extinction and evolution. To be too well adapted leads to evolutionary stagnation and extinction. To be stressed too much leads to death or rapid evolution.

There are problems with this idea. First, this edge of chaos has never been observed. Although this idea can be mathematically modeled, it has no basis in observable fact. It attempts to model the timing and patterns of extinction, but it doesn't provide the *why* of dinosaur extinction. Second, we have observable evidence that shows that dinosaurs were killed by water catastrophe. A worldwide flood is a better explanation of why so many dinosaurs were killed. Although chaos theory falls short of explaining dinosaur extinction, the biblical account seems to fit the facts.

Students may recognize the application to the concept of "punctuated equilibrium," which is the idea that life forms remain static, in equilibrium, until a catastrophe of some sort — biologic, geologic, environmental, or cosmic — causes the death of many and the rapid (punctuated) evolution of a few. Such a catastrophe would result in behavioral changes which would again affect the environment.

Advocates are fond of saying that "a butterfly flapping its wings in Beijing may cause a tornado in North America." But we all know this doesn't happen. It happens only in the world of computer simulations. In the real world, small changes are absorbed by the earth's much larger systems. The earth's marvelous design maintains its overall stability.

Biologic systems are likewise well designed, able to adapt to change. Such adaptations may be both physical and behavioral, but the adaptations are limited by genetic variability. If the environmental changes are too great, the species may go extinct, but no observation in the real world leads us to the conclusion that such pressures cause it to evolve into a different form.

II. HOW DO WE KNOW WHAT DINOSAURS WERE LIKE?

Using the scientific method, scientists employ the five senses to gather information. They collect facts, make measurements, run experiments, and study extensively before they arrive at a conclusion. The scientific method specifies that the measurements made and the experiments run today will give the same results tomorrow when anyone else does them. On the basis of these observations, conclusions can be made which are intended to arrive at truth. Does this method work in dinosaur research as well?

Unfortunately, since there are currently no dinosaurs to study, it is not possible to make measurements and run experiments on living specimens. All that remains of these fascinating creatures are fragmented fossils. Relatively few dinosaur skeletons have been found complete, or even nearly complete. Thousands of *pieces* of dinosaurs have been uncovered, but usually there are just bone fragments. While these fossils can be helpful in research, they don't reveal the whole story. Even so, scientists can still record much data about dinosaurs. They can weigh and measure the remains, test their composition and that of the soil and other specimens, make many observations of the locations, and compare data to other known facts. Based on fossil evidence scientists have been able to reach some reasonable conclusions.

How Big Were the Dinosaurs?

The term "dinosaur" usually evokes visions of enormous beasts. Yes, many dinosaurs were huge, but most were of a less extraordinary size. With bones identified from animals the size of a chicken, researchers know that some dinosaurs were quite small. The average size was  perhaps that of a hippopotamus or perhaps a little larger.

Did Dinosaurs Lay Eggs?

A few dinosaur eggs have been found, and thus we know that at least some dinosaurs laid eggs. Although this proves that *some* laid eggs, we must not assume that *all* dinosaurs laid eggs. Among several animal categories — mammals, reptiles, amphibians, and fish — there are creatures that lay eggs and others that bear live young. As far as we know, all birds lay eggs, but we aren't certain that all dinosaurs did so.

Cold-blooded or Warm-blooded?

By looking at dinosaur bones, many scientists have concluded that these creatures were cold-blooded animals whose body temperatures were dependent upon the environment. Today, there is a great deal of controversy over this. Dinosaur bones do not provide definitive information about this issue. Some dinosaur features seem to suggest dinosaurs were warm-blooded animals. Some scientists now claim that dinosaurs were warm-blooded when young and became cold-blooded as they grew into adulthood. How can they know this? The fossils just don't tell.

Did Dinosaurs Have Scaly Skin?

From the pile of bones left over from a chicken dinner, is it possible to discern the color the hen's — or rooster's — feathers were? If such knowledge were truly important, it could be obtained by researching from processor to producer, but with fossil relics, this procedure is unfeasible. It is impossible to determine the appearance and type of skin these creatures had by simply looking at dinosaur bones. Most scientists have concluded that the dinosaurs had scales like a reptile. On rare occasions, skin impressions have been preserved and appear scaly, though they are somewhat different from standard reptile scales. In spite of this find, many scientists (particularly those who argue for the warm-bloodedness of dinosaurs) insist that dinosaurs had hair like mammals, and a few others have speculated that these beasts had feathers like a bird. The direct fossil evidence suggests scales.

A chicken-sized dinosaur fossil has recently been found in China. According to early pictures, there are impressions along the fossil's spine that appeared to be short, downy feathers, less than a half-inch long. This fossil made big news at first, but once it was further scrutinized, it was determined that the "feathers" were just unusual fibers, probably embedded in the skin, but certainly not feathers. The initial rush to accept these as feathers underscores the tremendous, although questionable, interest in "proving" that dinosaurs evolved into birds.

What Did Dinosaurs Eat?

Most knowledge of dinosaur diets has been generated from comparisons of fossilized teeth to similar teeth in living creatures. Most of the dinosaurs appear to have been plant eaters with teeth and stomachs designed for digesting plant material. However, a few of them apparently ate meat, for they had long, sharp teeth which are typical of meat eaters.

While most of today's animals with

long sharp teeth eat meat, some do eat plants, so we can't unerringly decide this issue by looking at the fossilized teeth alone. To come to accurate conclusions, we need to interpret data found in the internal organs of the particular animals, but these are present only in living creatures, not fossils. Occasionally, the organs are found partially mummified, and in a few cases the stomach contents have been studied. The research of these fossils supports the idea that some dinosaurs ate meat, but when scientists can only study bones, it is difficult to determine exactly what each animal was like when it was alive.

What Do Fossils Show?

Dinosaur remains are rarely found intact, complete in themselves. It is very helpful when a complete skeleton is discovered, but in a typical fossil deposit, only a few bones may be present which are also disarticulated, disconnected, flattened, and ripped apart. In fact, particular fossil remains may be found in a pile with an assortment of other dinosaur bones. The excavation open to public viewing at Dinosaur National Monument (Colorado) is an excellent example of this. Although scientists usually work very carefully, the reconstruction of dinosaurs tends to be a very error-prone occupation, and some mistakes have been made.

These mistakes, although later acknowledged by paleontologists (those who study fossils), are very rarely corrected for the general public's knowledge. Consider the case of Tyrannosaurus Rex. In many movies as well as in children's books, Tyrannosaurus Rex is portrayed as a fierce killer. In fact, his name means "King Tyrant Lizard." Did you know that in recent times many scientists have downgraded Tyrannosaurus Rex from a killer to a scavenger? Most paleontologists feel that although this beast did eat meat, he probably ate creatures which had already died.

Scientists have come to this conclusion for several reasons. The anatomy of the T-Rex included two front legs that were so short they could neither touch each other nor reach his mouth. These legs would have been useless in a duel to the death with predator or prey. Although the dauntless dinosaur sported long and sharp teeth with serrated edges which could be replaced if dislodged, they appear to have been rather shallowly rooted in the jawbone and may have easily broken off. Also, if Tyrannosaurus Rex got into a fierce fight, it's possible that all his teeth would have fallen out. This new evidence has led many experts to conclude that he was not built for fighting, but for scavenging.

Dilophosaurs featured prominently in *Jurassic Park* are represented as brightly colored creatures. Actually, who knows? Many living reptiles possess beautiful skin colors and patterns — but dinosaur bones tell us nothing about hide color. The Dilophosaurs in the movie also spit poison. However, bones do not spit; therefore, we have no means of knowing if the living dinosaur had this theatrical capability.

How Fast Could Dinosaurs Move?

Dinosaurs were once described as slow-moving beasts, much like lethargic crocodiles basking in the sun. However, recent studies have revealed evidence of dinosaurs' extensive movement and agility. Since fossil footprints were made while the

creature lived, much can be learned about dinosaur behavior through their study. Fossilized dinosaur footprints occasionally show stride length, which suggests the ability to run. Now scientists speculate that some of these creatures could run quite fast, and others could leap like kangaroos.

How Intelligent Were the Dinosaurs?

Velociraptor is portrayed on screen as a vicious killer which hunted in packs. The dinosaur's fossils do have intimidating teeth and claws, but paleontologists cannot know with any certainty that these animals hunted in groups. They were depicted as highly intelligent, able to reason, manipulate door handles, stalk their prey, and even able to learn more effective ways of hunting prey. While Velociraptor's brain size was large compared to other dinosaurs, that would not necessarily guarantee any degree of problem-solving intellect. Brain *size* is not the determining factor for intelligence — brain *organization* is much more significant.

Scientists cannot make generalizations about brain organization by looking exclusively at the skull. However, even Raptor's cranial capacity was not exceptional. Evolutionists who assume that modern birds evolved from upright, two-legged dinosaurs, also conclude that the smartest dinosaur would have had less brain power than an ostrich, one of the world's least intelligent animals. Certainly this bird does not have the abilities that Hollywood attributed to Velociraptor!

How Did Dinosaurs Behave?

Reconstructing dinosaur behavior is a difficult task. Fossils are not "photographs" of dinosaur life. There is no way to know, just by looking at a bone or a collection of bones, if a dinosaur was nurturing, as some say, or if it exhibited any other particular behavioral characteristics.

Based on discoveries of dinosaur egg clutches, some scientists have speculated that, on occasion, mother dinosaurs cared for their eggs and for their young after hatching, similar to the way some modern alligators do. Some dinosaur hatchlings with pieces of eggshells have been found in the nest, with adult dinosaur fossils nearby. It appears to some as if the mother dinosaur was near the nest when both were suddenly buried. Whether or not the adult dinosaur was a nurturing parent with offspring or a hungry cannibalizing relative cannot be determined.

When we see fossils together, what do we really know?

Do we know that they were living together when they died? Can we even know for certain that they died in that location? All we can know is that they were buried together. Trying to reconstruct the past, based on the partial evidence found in the present, is risky business, and the history of dinosaur speculations is littered with many discarded ideas once clung to with determination.

III. WHAT MAKES DINOSAURS UNIQUE?

Although we are unable to study a live dinosaur, most scientists have concluded that the dinosaurs were a special category of reptile. They appear to have been cold-blooded, egg-laying, scale-covered beasts. The animals alive today who have those characteristics are reptiles, and therefore scientists have concluded that dinosaurs were a special category of reptile.

Although we cannot study live dinosaurs today, we can study reptiles. All reptiles have scales as opposed to hair or feathers. All are cold-blooded. Most lay eggs, although not all do. Some reptiles are meat eaters, and some are plant eaters. Various species have long, sharp teeth, while others have no teeth at all.

Dinosaur Hips

What sets dinosaurs apart from the reptiles we see today is primarily their hip structure and the fact that they lived on land. Dinosaurs had hips that placed their legs beneath them, like a cow or an ostrich. These hips designate erect stance. Two different types of dinosaur hips have been recognized. One is called the "lizard hip" and the other is called the "bird hip." Today's reptiles have legs that come off the sides of their bodies and then down, such as a crocodile or a lizard. Birds have a slightly different hip structure as well, although they do stand erect. As far as is known, there are no animals alive today which have either a "lizard hip" or a "bird hip." Only extinct dinosaurs had these types of hip structure.

Dinosaur Skulls

Another distinguishing feature of the dinosaur is the structure of their skulls. All dinosaurs had skulls with peculiar openings in the sides. There are a few animals alive today (such as the tuatara in New Zealand) which have these peculiar openings in their skulls, but even these do not have a "lizard hip" or a "bird hip" and thus are not considered dinosaurs. In order to be classified as such, the animal must have either "lizard hips" or "bird hips," along with holes in its skull.

Other Ancient Giant Reptiles

Some of our favorite giant "prehistoric" reptiles were not really dinosaurs. The Plesiosaur which swam in the oceans was a giant reptile. Technically, this creature was not a dinosaur because it didn't live on land and possess "lizard hips" or "bird hips." These marine animals had flipper-like paddles rather than legs. All dinosaurs were, by definition, land-dwelling animals. Many of the true dinosaurs probably spent time in swamps, lakes, rivers, or along the shoreline, but like today's crocodiles, were quite at home on land.

Flying reptiles like the Pteranodon or the Pterodactyl were not truly dinosaurs either. They are classified as giant flying reptiles, because they did not have the correct hip structure to be dinosaurs. Animals such as Dimetrodon, with its huge sail fin, was not grouped with the dinosaurs either. Dimetrodon had the typical reptile leg sprawl, with legs coming off the side, and is classed as a "mammal-like" reptile.

IV. IS THERE EVIDENCE THAT DINOSAURS EVOLVED FROM ANOTHER KIND OF CREATURE?

If evolution really happened, then the dinosaurs obviously had to evolve from other creatures — from amphibians, from fish, and from single-celled creatures before that. However, the evidence for this claim is missing. When dinosaurs are found in the fossil record, they are fully dinosaur. The fossil record shows dinosaurs to be fully operational, fully functional. They have all the marvelous characteristics typical of dinosaurs. Never do we see any evidence that these creatures evolved from something else.

To support evolutionary theory, a particular dinosaur's physical feature would need to show evidence of a process of change. For instance, if a fish had changed into an amphibian, there would have been a transition between water-filtering gill and an air-breathing, lung-like apparatus. If a swimming creature had changed into a walking animal, there would have been some kind of transition from fins to legs. Thus a half-fin/half-leg should be found, as would a half-gill/half-lung. Evidence of this type of transition should be seen in the fossil record, but none has been found.

The many different types of dinosaurs possessed a variety of traits. We find some dinosaurs with spiked tails and plated spines. We find dinosaurs with long necks and some with short necks. We find some with nostrils on top of the heads, and others with nostrils on the snout. We find dinosaurs with gigantic hind legs and dwarfed front legs. We find some of these creatures with huge jaws and sharp teeth, and others with flat teeth. But every time we find a dinosaur, each characteristic appears to have been fully functional, designed to do just what it did. There is *no* evidence that any dinosaur changed into another dinosaur, or that any of them came from some non-dinosaur.

Likewise, there is no evidence that dinosaurs evolved

into anything else. Some scientists are glib in their pronouncements that dinosaurs became birds. Some scientists even say that birds *are* dinosaurs. In reality, there is a great deal of difference between these two categories, and the evidence cited is very slight.

What about Archaeopteryx?

The classic fossil used to support the theory that reptiles evolved into birds is the extinct creature called Archaeopteryx. It's true that this creature possesses some features typical of reptiles and some traits of

birds, but each characteristic was fully formed. It had fully formed teeth, like reptiles, and while some fossil birds also had teeth, modern birds don't have teeth. However, not all reptiles have teeth. Therefore, this cannot be a determinative characteristic.

Archaeopteryx was a winged creature, and its breast bone was more typical of reptile than bird. Archaeopteryx had grasping feet as if it could perch in a tree, like a bird, as opposed to running on the ground. It had claws on its wings, but several modern birds successfully utilize such claws.

Most particularly, Archaeopteryx had fully formed feathers — bird feathers. Feathers are extremely complex features, and this creature was fully feathered. Some evolutionists claim that reptilian scales became frayed, and then became feathers. However, feathers are not merely frayed scales. Feathers have elaborate, interlocking barbs and barbules which keep them wind and water resistant. Feathers are *not* frayed scales. Feathers have been designed with a complex structure, for a specific purpose, to perform a special job.

The evidence indicates that Archaeopteryx was not a transitional form between reptiles and birds. Rather, Archaeopteryx was a rare bird, now extinct.

Would a Transition Survive?

How could a walking, ground-dwelling — or even tree-dwelling — reptile become a bird that could fly? For the front limbs to be effective wings, multiple mutations would have to result in progressively longer fingers or arms with a membrane between each finger. Long before the walking or climbing creature would have good wings, it would have inadequate legs and would be at a tremendous disadvantage against predators. In fact, it is hard to imagine how a creature that could not yet fly, but which possessed long fingers or arms, could even survive, let alone have an advantage in the struggle for existence. Natural selection would weed out these mutant misfits.

Furthermore, the breathing apparatuses of birds and reptiles are entirely different. In birds, air flows in one air pipe and out another, while in reptiles, the air goes in and out through the same opening, as in mammals. Since breathing is essential for survival, and cannot be halted for even a few minutes, how could such a major transition occur by mutation and natural selection? A similar problem exists with the totally different design of the heart. Clearly birds did not evolve from dinosaurs or other reptiles.

The final blow to this evolutionary idea comes with the recognition that a variety of bird fossils appears in the fossil record at about the same stratigraphic level — perhaps even lower — than dinosaurs, along with Archaeopteryx. Recognizing that a lower level means an earlier burial, we can be sure that these birds could not have evolved from dinosaurs. They appear fully formed and fully bird, right from their first appearance.

Did Reptiles Evolve to Mammals?

Many evolutionists talk about a transition between reptiles and mammals, pointing to a category of animal called "mammal-like reptiles." The Dimetrodon, a creature with a sail fin along its backbone, usually assumed in popular literature to be a dinosaur, was actually a mammal-like reptile. It was a reptile that had some features suggestive of mammals. Evolutionists don't claim that dinosaurs evolved into mammals. In evolutionary thinking, the mammals evolved from these mammal-like reptiles at about the same time that dinosaurs evolved.

There are several different categories of unusual mammal-like reptiles. Evolutionists think that only one of these animals survived and evolved into rodent-like mammals, which then evolved into the wide range of mammals we see today. The rest of the mammal-like reptiles became extinct.

Interestingly, various mammal-like reptiles, all evolving separately, supposedly developed the same mammal-like features at the same time. This "parallel" evolution is even more statistically unlikely than evolution itself. Actually, even evolutionists admit the unlikely nature of evolution at all. For the same thing to have happened several times in exactly the same pattern becomes unthinkably unlikely, and the evidence cited in support of this transition is extremely weak.

I believe we can say with confidence that dinosaurs were dinosaurs from the start; they didn't evolve *from* anything else nor did they evolve *into* anything else.

V. WHEN DID DINOSAURS LIVE?

The evolutionary reconstruction of history places dinosaurs as living from about 220 million years ago (estimates vary) to about 65 million years ago when they became extinct. Scientists have chosen these dates by studying rocks and fossils in the present. However, it is not the best reconstruction of history. The reconstruction which better fits the scientific evidence is found in Scripture which says all the basic categories of animals were created during the six days of creation week.

Creation in Six Days

According to the biblical account of creation, on day one God created the heavens, the earth, and then light on the earth. On day two of creation week, He formed both the oceans and the atmosphere and an environment in which life could thrive. Then the next day, after forming the continents, He caused plant life to grow on those continents. On the fourth day, He created the sun and the moon, those features necessary for life on earth. By day five, the planet was prepared for living creatures, and so God created life for the oceans. He also created birds. On the sixth day of creation week, He created land animals. Of course, the creation was climaxed by the creation of His image in man on day six.

Day Five — Dragons

And God said, Let the waters bring forth abundantly the moving creature that hath life, and fowl that may fly above the earth in the open firmament of heaven. And God created great whales, and every living creature that moveth, which the waters brought forth abundantly, after their kind, and every winged fowl after his kind: and God saw that it was good. And God blessed them, saying, Be fruitful, and multiply, and fill the waters in the seas, and let fowl multiply in the earth (Gen. 1:20–22).

Where did the dinosaurs fit? When talking about the creation of ocean creatures, the Bible says that God created the great "whales" (King James Version) or great "sea monsters" (New American Standard). The Hebrew word translated *whales* or *sea monsters* is actually the Hebrew word that means "dragons." So, this verse tells us that God created great dragons for life in the ocean.

The ancient legends of dragons — huge reptilian beasts with long necks and plated spines — depict beasts very similar to our modern reconstruction of dinosaurs. Mariners have told of dragons in the oceans even up until recent times. Almost every culture around the globe has legends of dragons, and these legends show striking similarities.

Some dragon stories recorded in human history involve people who actually did exist. Alexander the Great encountered dinosaur-like beasts, and so did King Beowulf of the British Isles. The ancient historian Berosus wrote of such beasts. Clearly, something that fits our modern ideas of dinosaurs existed in human history.

It is possible that the legends of dragons are actually the faded memories of human encounters with dinosaurs. Certainly, if an individual encountered a dinosaur, he would tell his children, who would tell their children, and on down the line. Perhaps the story would get bigger and better through the embellishment of telling and retelling, but the essence of the story would remain.

Dragons are reputed to have lived up through the Middle Ages when brave knights would slay such fierce beasts. The scientific listings of animals of that day included dragons as rare, but still living creatures. We can conclude that dragons did exist but that they eventually joined the ranks of the extinct.

Day Six and Land Animals

And God said, Let the earth bring forth the living creature after his kind, cattle, and creeping thing, and beast of the earth after his kind: and it was so. And God made the beast of the earth after his kind, and cattle after their kind, and every thing that creepeth upon the earth after his kind: and God saw that it was good (Gen. 1:24–25).

On day six, the Bible mentions that God created "the beasts of the earth" and "the creeping things" and "the cattle." The "creeping things" obviously were small animals, and, of course, many of the dinosaurs were small, "creeping" animals. Others were the "beasts of the earth" or the "beasts of the field." These would be the larger animals, and certainly many of the dinosaurs were quite large. The "cattle" were the domesticated animals. We can only speculate as to whether or not dinosaurs were domesticated. Because most reptiles don't make very good pets, and they usually live in different habitats than do people, we can conclude that there were probably few, if any, domesticated dinosaurs.

The Bible tells us some other important things. At the end of Genesis, chapter 1, when creation was finished, God commanded all of the animals to be plant eaters (Gen. 1:30). As Creator, God had the authority to set the rules over His creation. He knew what He wanted, and He knew how everything was designed. In the original creation there was to have been no carnivorous activity — no death, no bloodshed, no meat eating. Even the dinosaurs were all to be herbivores when they were first created. All creatures were to live forever in perfect harmony. It was all "very good" (Gen. 1:31).

VI. HOW DID THE DINOSAURS ACQUIRE THEIR CHARACTERISTICS?

By the time of the great flood recorded in Genesis 7, it appears that some of the dinosaurs were meat eaters. Actually, we don't know for *sure* they were carnivorous, because all we see now are bits and pieces of bones of creatures, some of whom appear to have been meat eaters.

Assuming that some of them did eat meat, what happened? How did they acquire their taste for meat and acquire

their long sharp teeth? How did they develop digestive systems seemingly designed for carnivorous activity? What happened between the time of creation, when they were created to eat plants, and the time of the flood, at which time it appears that some animals ate meat?

The answer is found in Genesis, chapter 3, where we see that Adam and Eve rebelled against the Creator's authority and plan for their lives. They chose, when tempted by Satan, to set their own rules. God had told Adam and Eve, "Of every tree of the garden thou mayest freely eat: but of the Tree of the Knowledge of Good and Evil, thou shalt not eat of it: for in the day thou eatest thereof thou shalt surely die" (Gen. 2:16–17).

As we read in the New Testament, "The wages of sin is death" (Rom. 6:23). And the penalty was no different in the beginning. God had promised that death would be the result of their disobedience, but "The serpent said unto the woman, ye shall not surely die . . . ye shall be as gods" (Gen. 3:4–5). Adam and Eve chose to rebel against God, thus incurring His punishment. "For dust thou art, and unto dust thou shalt return" (Gen. 3:19).

The Curse

As Creator, God has the authority to set the guidelines for proper living for His created beings, and to set the penalty of death of creation for Adam's sin; this is called the "Curse" in Scripture.

Not only were Adam and Eve cursed at this time, the entire creation was cursed. We see that Adam and Eve's bodies were changed (Gen. 3:16–17,19). The plant kingdom was cursed (v.14), and the entire earth came under this punishment (v.17), but at the same time, God promised to provide a means to restore creation. This promise was fulfilled when Jesus, God's Son, came to earth.

Many changes in creation resulted from the Fall and the Curse. Not only did death become a universal principle, in which people die, animals die, plants wither and fade, elements decay, stars burn out, etc., but "the whole creation is groaning and travailing in pain together until now" (Rom. 8:20). Because of Adam and Eve's rebellion, the second law of thermodynamics was put in motion.

From "Very Good" to "Violence"

Evidently, some time after the Curse, certain animals acquired a taste for meat and carnivorous activity abounded. Certainly death reigned because, just a few generations later in the days of Noah, we see that "the earth was filled with violence through them [the violent inhabitants]; and, behold, I will destroy them with the earth" (Gen. 6:13). This is primarily talking about human violence, but why not animal violence as well? After all, the earth was full of violent activity!

Somehow then, between the time of the Curse and the flood, things changed. The Bible doesn't give us all the details but we can speculate on the possibilities.

(1) It may be that God originally created animals with offensive and defensive characteristics and the body style for eating meat, knowing that soon creation would be altered and they would need them.

(2) Perhaps at the time of the Curse, He loosened some of the genetic controls that would allow animals to alter and adapt to their new situation including certain body style changes. Today's DNA system has become fixed so that major changes can no longer occur.

(3) It may be that some of these characteristics were inspired and accomplished by Satan himself. We know that Satan was in a rage toward God and toward His creation and wanted to do what he could to destroy or pollute it. He especially wanted to alter humankind so the Redeemer promised in Genesis 3:15 could not come from the line of Eve. We know that Satan is a very intelligent being and may have been able to accomplish major genetic engineering either through actual gene splicing or perhaps through selective breeding.

(4) It may be that God performed genetic engineering at

this point. To change a rose with no thorns into a rose with thorns takes a DNA alteration. To change a crawling animal into a slithering snake takes DNA alteration, as it does with Eve's body style change. It may be that God altered creation to forever remind Adam and Eve of the awful "wages of sin." Every time they saw one animal kill another they regretted their sinful choice.

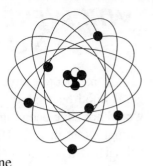

We don't have all the details, but we do know that within just a few generations the earth was full of violence and also that there were "giants in the earth in those days" (Gen. 6:4). It is this violent, distorted world that we see preserved in the fossil record. It is not the world as God created it but a world perverted and destroyed by sin.

VII. HOW DID DINOSAURS GO EXTINCT?

There's a new "dinosaur extinction theory-of-the-month club" these days, with many scientists engaging in wild speculations. No consensus exists because most scientists deny biblical history as true history and thus are trapped in wrong thinking.

God wisely recorded a momentous event in world history in Genesis chapters six through nine. God's justice demanded that the wicked world of Noah's day be destroyed, and the flood was the instrument by which He accomplished His just purposes. The resulting flood was so destructive that no land inhabitants could have survived without God's provision for them on board Noah's ark.

Dinosaur fossils lie buried in sedimentary rock strata laid down as muddy sediments by the flood of Noah's day, rife with the remains of plants and animals which died in the flood. The sediments hardened into sedimentary rock and the dead things became fossils. Obviously, then, most of the dinosaurs died in the great flood.

VIII. WERE DINOSAURS ON NOAH'S ARK?

Some people have doubted the biblical account of the great flood because they believe the ark, as built by Noah, would not have been big enough to take two of every kind of animal. Note that the Bible does not say that every kind of animal had to be represented on board, but only those "in whose nostrils was the breath of life of all that was in the dry land" (Gen. 7:22). Oceanic creatures — the fish, the whales, and the marine reptiles — did not have to be on board. These creatures would have survived (at least in representative numbers) outside the ark, even though the majority of each probably died. Air-breathing, land-dwelling creatures had to be on board the ark to survive the flood.

God commanded Noah to allow two of every kind, or category, of animal on board the ark for their survival. Since dinosaurs were land-dwellers and air-breathers, they must have been on board.

Was the Ark Large Enough?

Noah's ark was immense. The biblical dimensions are approximately 450 feet long, 75 feet wide, and 45 feet high; in all, about one-and-one-half *million* cubic feet. It was

an enormous vessel. Still, if Noah had to take the two biggest Brachiosaurs he could find, the ark would have filled up quickly. Was there enough room for the dinosaurs as well as the other animals?

To answer this question, we must answer two others. First, how many categories of dinosaurs were there? Second, what was their average size?

How Many Types of Dinosaurs Were There?

Modern paleontologists have discovered and named about 600 dinosaur species, but many of these species are based on the discovery of pieces of bone, *not* an entire skeleton. If a bone is found in a differ- ent loca- tion or in a differ- ent layer of rock than other similar bones, that fossil will be given a new species name. Thus, there are probably many more named species than there were true categories of dinosaur. It may very well be that there were no more than 50 categories of dinosaur and perhaps even quite a few less. Dinosaurs like Apatosaurus, Brachiosaurus, S u p e r s a u r u s , Ultrasaurus, and Diplodocus, may all have been in the same created category. They

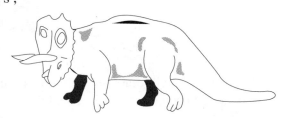

were all very similar and the differences may have been just a variation among individuals or local adaptations, much like the various breeds of cattle or dogs we see today.

Were the Largest Dinosaurs on Board?

Another interesting thing to note is that modern reptiles are not like mammals. While all dinosaurs started out as eggs, or at least small newborns, reptiles continue to grow larger as long as they live. The largest Galapagos sea turtle is the oldest Galapagos sea turtle. The largest crocodile is the oldest crocodile. Remember that before the flood, the Bible says that humans lived almost a thousand years. If dinosaurs lived a thousand years and grew larger each year of their lives, they would become quite large! It is possible that the very large Brachiosaurs were actually very old and not even typical adult size.

God would not have wanted to bring onto the ark the two largest Brachiosaurs on earth, because those would have been the oldest Brachiosaurs. The purpose of the ark was for survival and species propagation of its occupants after the flood. It would have been advantageous to choose young, strong specimens which would be able to survive the rigors of the trip and reproduce afterwards. If the Brachiosaurs chosen were the size of a hippopotamus, there was plenty of room on the ark for the various categories of dinosaur, the mammals, birds, reptiles, and amphibians, as well as Noah and his family.

Did Dinosaurs Survive the Flood?

This, of course, means that dinosaurs survived the flood and would have left the ark with the other animals going into the new post-flood world. This new world would have had a very different environment than before the flood. As a result, dinosaurs as well as other creatures have evidently become extinct since that time.

Theories on dinosaur extinction are many and varied. The most widely publicized evolutionary theory is the idea of a comet or asteroid crashing into the earth and starting a chain reaction which eventually led to the extinction of all the dinosaurs. Other extinction theories are even more far-fetched.

This issue is very complex. Whatever killed the dinosaurs and many of the marine reptiles at the same time was survived by many other marine and land animals as well as plants. How could tiny, fragile birds or mammals survive an event which killed all the large, strong dinosaurs?

What Does the Bible Say?

Undoubtedly the best explanation for dinosaur extinction is the biblical model of history. Entering a very different world after the flood, dinosaurs probably found themselves at a disadvantage. Before the flood, plants were larger, vegetation was lush, and many dinosaurs were big eaters. After the flood, plants were less abundant, and many areas of the world were environmentally harsh. The dinosaurs just didn't seem to make it. Many different animal kinds went extinct during the centuries following the flood.

The Ice Age, which followed the flood, caused life to be even more impossible for cold-blooded reptiles. Remarkably, dinosaur fossils have recently been discovered in glaciated areas like the Arctic and Antarctic. These areas are totally uninhabitable today by cold-blooded animals. Obviously, things are quite different now than they were in the past.

We can also speculate that if the dragons described in legends were really dinosaurs, there may have been a concerted effort by humans to kill them off. We know that other large animals were hunted to extinction by Ice Age dwellers. The conclusion is that dinosaurs did not survive long and appear to have gone extinct.

These mighty creatures did not disappear from the earth, however, before they had been observed by Noah's descendants after the flood. In South America, Africa, China, Australia, Europe, North America, and elsewhere, man engraved on rock walls the images of dinosaur-like beasts.

Two such pictographs can be seen in the Grand Canyon

and several in Utah. The engravings are on rock walls which also contain carvings of buffalo, antelope, and mountain lions. These animals are native to North America, and these pictures also show animals like mammoths and camels, which have long been extinct on this continent although they left skeletal clues to their existence.

IX. WHAT DO THE DINOSAUR FOSSILS TEACH US ABOUT THE FLOOD?

The dinosaur fossils, indeed all other known fossils, too, seem to show that the event which deposited them was an unthinkably catastrophic event, worldwide in scope. Sedimentary rock, by definition, is made of water-deposited sediments which have hardened into rock. These sediments are the type of strata that would have resulted from a huge flood such as that described in Genesis.

Where Are Dinosaur Fossils Found?

Typically, fossils are found in fossil graveyards where the animals have been dismembered and the remains broken and scattered about. The bones are mixed with bones of other individual animals, making reconstruction extremely difficult. Animal and plant remains from vastly different environments and habitats are often mixed together. For instance, the dominant fossil at Dinosaur National Monument Park is a fossil clam. Many times, the deposits in which the fossils are found cover great areas on the earth's surface — at times hundreds of thousands of square miles. The event which deposited these sediments was not only of large geographic extent, but involved intense energy levels. Truly, what could have been larger and more powerful than the worldwide flood?

Dinosaur fossils are found on every continent, including the polar regions. Many of the best dinosaur fossil deposits (at least those that have been best studied) are found in the western United States and, to a lesser degree, in western Canada. One very interesting deposit in Montana contains portions of up to ten thousand duck-billed dinosaurs fossilized together. According to evolutionists, these fossils were buried by a catastrophic event of extreme magnitude, extensive in area and impact.

For any creature to be fossilized in a flood, it must be buried rapidly. Otherwise, it will decompose or be eaten within a fairly short period of time. Obviously, these vast fossil graveyards were collections of creatures who died in the global flood of Noah's day.

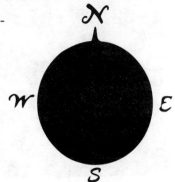

X. WHY DOESN'T THE BIBLE MENTION DINOSAURS?

The word "dinosaur" wasn't coined until the 1850s after dinosaur fossils were rediscovered, so the word "dinosaur" is not mentioned in the Bible. However, dinosaur-like creatures *are* mentioned in Scripture. As we have seen, the Bible mentions dragons, even in the creation account. There are many other places where the Bible talks about both land and sea dragons as if they were real beasts (Ps. 74:13, 91:13; Isa. 13:22, 34:13, etc.) Even flying reptiles are mentioned in Scripture (Isa. 14:29, 30:6).

The most important biblical passages that describe dinosaur-like beasts are found in the Book of Job. Job lived relatively soon after the flood, probably before the time of Abraham. If dinosaurs aboard Noah's ark survived the flood, they would probably have been alive in Job's day. In chapters 38 through 41, God himself talks to Job, and He points out various aspects of creation. The two most startling examples of His creative majesty are called behemoth (40:15) and leviathan (41:1).

Behemoth

Behemoth was an incredibly large, grass-eating (Job 40:15) beast, with a huge girth (v.16) and a tail that looked like a cedar tree (v. 17). He had very strong bones (v.18) and was the "chief of the ways of God" (v. 19). Evidently behemoth was the biggest land animal that God created. He was a dweller in swampy regions (v. 20–22) and was afraid of nothing (v. 23–24). The description appears to fit the large sauropods as reconstructed from their fossils, such as Apatosaurus.

Leviathan

Leviathan in Job, chapter 41, is described as a marine creature (v. 1, 7) that spent at least some of its time on land (v. 26–30). He was incredibly fierce (v. 10), with large teeth (v. 14) and scales (v. 15–17). This beast was so vicious that he was even compared to Satan himself (Isa. 27:1). Most remarkable is his ability to breath fire (v. 18–21). Perhaps this gives us a clue as to the fire-breathing dragon legends of the past.

Today, we may wonder how an animal could have breathed fire, but actually, a fire-breathing dinosaur is not impossible. The chemistry necessary to achieve this feat is not nearly as complicated as that possessed by other animals today, such as the firefly, the electric eel, and others. Most dinosaurs were big plant eaters. The digestion of plant material produces methane gas, which can burn. A methane belch only needs a spark to ignite it.

Several known chemicals which burst into flame in the presence of oxygen would be able to provide the necessary spark if combined with methane. Produc-ing these chemicals in living things would not be out of the question. Per-haps some dinosaurs had glands which could secrete these chemicals, which when combined with oxygen and methane, would produce a power-ful flame thrower! Since we've never observed such a beast, we can't know for certain, but the bib-lical account makes sense out of the legends of "fire-breathing drag-ons."

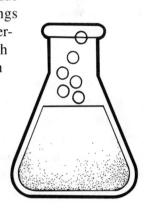

XI. ARE THERE ANY DINOSAURS STILL LIVING TODAY?

From these dragon legends, we can surmise that dragons (or dinosaurs) lived until fairly recent times. We are not able to say that they still exist, although there are a few rare and tantalizing developments that cause us to wonder.

Marine dragons have been reported by sailors, up through World War II and even yet today. The Loch Ness monster and other sightings of unidentified creatures in various inland lakes may provide a clue. We don't know what these creatures are, but it is possible they are some sort of giant reptiles— per-haps Plesiosaurs — which lived in the water.

Even today, the huge oceans are relatively unexplored and new animal species are discovered from time to time. Perhaps giant marine creatures have survived in isolated ar-eas.

Another hint comes from a discovery in 1977. A Japanese fishing trawler netted the rotting carcass of an animal off the coast of New Zealand. This carcass was huge and unlike any that the sailors had ever seen. Samples of the flesh were inconclusive, but in the sketches and photographs taken, the creature appears to resemble a Plesiosaur more than any other known creature. It certainly doesn't look like either a basking shark or whale. A possible explanation is that this was a recently deceased Plesiosaur that had survived undetected in the ocean. Unfortunately, the carcass was disposed of at sea and is not available for study, but we can assume that it must have been part of a larger family in order to have survived.

There are also rumors of reptilian beasts still living in isolated rain forests, both in Africa and South America. Natives describe these beasts with great similarity to modern reconstructions of dinosaurs. Indeed, when they are shown sketches of dinosaurs drawn from fossil remains they identify the beasts that they have seen as Sauropods. Expeditions to verify these rumors have not been successful, although they have produced additional, fascinating clues. Further expeditions are planned, and may be more successful.

In summary, it is incorrect to make definite claims of dinosaurs living today. More research needs to be done, but perhaps living dinosaurs may one day be discovered. Then we could *know the facts* about dinosaur habits and characteristics.

Even if dinosaurs are discovered, however, this would *not* disprove evolution. It would be difficult to accommodate into evolution, but evolution is a very flexible concept and can be molded to include almost any discovery.

XII. CAN DINOSAURS BE CLONED FROM FOSSIL DNA?

The dinosaurs in both *Jurassic Park* movies were produced by cloning. Their DNA was obtained from fossilized insects which had bitten living dinosaurs long ago. The dinosaur DNA was contained inside the insects which were fossilized in amber. Cloning technology has advanced in many ways in the last decade, bringing technology to a level never before obtained. We now know that it is possible to clone large animals, and the technology involved in this process is progressing rapidly. Without a doubt, cloning will become common in the future.

How Is Cloning Accomplished?

The process of cloning begins with the removal of the nucleus of a reproductive cell (that portion of the cell which contains the DNA code) and replacing the original nucleus with a nucleus from another cell of a *different* individual of the *same* species. The DNA proceeds to accomplish its created purpose, namely the development of the cell into a fetus, into a newborn, into an adult. In theory, the donor of the nucleus would see its exact replica develop in the denucleated host cell.

Several factors must be in place in order to accomplish cloning:

1. The entire DNA strand must be present in the donor source. This might be from a living or (potentially) fossilized source, but the DNA must be complete and without deterioration.

2. A host egg cell (or an egg) which can be denucleated must exist. The host nucleus must then be removed and the donor DNA inserted. This host

cell must be a living egg cell, obviously from a living organism. In animals, this implies a living female.

    3. The donated DNA must be from the same species as the host or biological reaction will cease.

Unfortunately, when cloning attempts are made, very often the offspring develop serious deformities and the egg ceases to grow. When an adult sheep was recently cloned, dozens of abnormalities occurred in many fetal sheep before a successful cloning was made, placing severe limitations on the economic feasibility of cloning. In all likelihood, however, technological advances will make cloning of living plants and animals commonplace in future decades.

Many have already called for a ban on human cloning, foreseeing a multitude of potential abuses. Unfortunately, egocentric or power hungry individuals will predictably soon attempt to do so.

Can Extinct Dinosaurs Be Cloned?

Cloning from fossil DNA is an entirely different matter. We know from laboratory tests that DNA, the library of information containing directions to build the organism, breaks down of its own accord. Without the protection and repair mechanisms of a living cell, the DNA

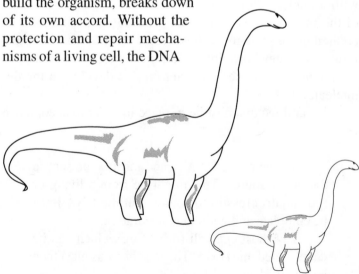

will not retain information for very long. Even under optimum conditions in experiments, DNA could not possibly survive more than ten thousand years or so.

In the evolutionary scenario, dinosaurs are thought to have lived from 220 to 65 million years ago. Thus, any fossilized DNA would supposedly be that old. It simply could not have survived. Even in a flood perspective, with the fossils being only a few thousand years old, it would be remarkable if major portions of DNA remained.

Recently, DNA has been recovered from ancient bone and plant material, including insects preserved in amber. Usually, the fragments found are only a portion of one gene, and yet each organism needs the information contained in many thousands of genes to grow and survive! To find *any* preserved DNA fits much better with the recent creation and flood view of history than it does the evolutionary view. Realistically, though, the cloning of large creatures from fossilized DNA will never happen.

On all these counts, we can see that cloning of dinosaurs will, in all likelihood, never happen.

XIII. WHAT IS THE MAIN MESSAGE OF THE JURASSIC PARK MOVIES?

As mentioned before, evolution theory occupies only a small part of screen time in the *Jurassic Park* movies. Rather, evolution is assumed, and it is assumed that all movie-viewers are thoroughly steeped in evolutionary thinking. Thus, the movie becomes an effective tool for promoting evolution. No credible person would dare question "science." However, many details are "science fiction," at best. Nevertheless, the science fiction does serve as an effective backdrop for a film with thriller chase scenes and horror dramatics.

One prominent theme was expressed by the repeated adage "Life will find a way." Naturalism, the belief that natural processes and events have produced complex life in the world, is obviously a philosophical position — a religion, as it were. Naturalism stands in contrast to supernaturalism, the belief that a supernatural God created all things and oversees their present life.

This illustrates how we should view origins and historical reconstructions. Both natural and supernatural are religious perspectives, and both will form the basis for scientific investigation and interpretation. Since both are ways of thinking, particularly as they relate to the unobserved past, neither can be proven or disproved. The scientific method, requiring observation, testing, repeatability, and falsifiability, cannot pass judgment on ideas about the past, particularly unobserved, one-time events. Evolution and creation are the origins doctrines of the two religious views, naturalism and supernaturalism, respectively.

When viewed in this manner, one recognizes that *Jurassic Park*'s main purpose (besides providing viewers with thrilling entertainment and producers with thrilling financial proceeds) was to promote a particular worldview.

What Is the Main Message of *The Lost World*?

The novel (which the 1997 movie was based upon) *The Lost World*, sequel to *Jurassic Park*, continued the theme of cloned dinosaurs running wild. Evolution was much more prominent, including a frank discussion of the weaknesses of the theory. However, evolution itself was not called into question. These serious problems were claimed to be solved through fanciful mathematical constructions of chaos theory.

Herein arises a great paradox. Evolutionists have publicly boasted that the second law of thermodynamics posed no problem for evolution. But now, well-respected evolutionists from the Santa Fe Institute (a scientific think tank) brag of a theory which solves this same (yet non-existent?) problem.

In reality, the problem of the second law is real and devastating to evolution theory. Computer simulations of order from chaos should never be allowed to substitute for observation. True evolutionary changes have never been observed, nor has the second law ever been violated.

What's Next for Chaos Theory?

We can already see a shift in chaos theory. Today, advocates focus on the pattern of complexity in a system, not just its origin. Creationists find this new "complexity theory" quite interesting, for they have consistently pointed out the amazing complexity of even a "simple" cell, or even a protein molecule, which far transcends the ability of mere natural processes to generate or improve. The next few years will be interesting, as evolutionists acknowledge these amazing design features.

Unfortunately, the recognition that natural processes are unable to produce complexity does not necessarily lead one to embrace creation thinking. As many abandon naturalism, they gravitate to the New Age movement, in which "Mother Nature" lives and produces complex life systems by design.

We can best understand both chaos theory and complexity theory as man's desperate attempt to deal with the reality of intricate life, while rejecting a personal Creator to whom one is responsible.

XIV. SO WHAT? WHAT DOES ALL THIS MEAN TO ME?

While we can't prove or disprove either evolution or creation, we can compare the positions and see which one is better supported by scientific evidence. As we have briefly shown, *all* the evidence regarding life in general and dinosaurs in particular fits very nicely in the creation model, while some evidence doesn't fit at all in the evolutionary view of the past, thus forcing evolutionists to adopt even more astounding ideas.

For instance, evolution can't allow the dragon legends to relate to dinosaurs, yet the legends which fit the descriptions of dinosaurs are found on every continent and among every people. Is this, as evolutionists label it, "collective imagination"? Creation insists that all people alive today descended from Noah and his family, and *they saw* dinosaurs!

Secondly, the possibility of dinosaurs living today would

force a serious revision of evolutionary thinking. What is the Loch Ness monster? What was the carcass found in 1977? What are the natives in Africa reporting? Evolution can't easily handle these things, but creation would expect them.

What of biblical evidence? Atheistic skeptics scoffingly dismiss the Bible; nevertheless, the Bible has been accepted as the Word of God through the centuries. Even today, most Americans accept it as an accurate guide to meaningful life. It has been analyzed, scrutinized, and tested, and found to be trustworthy — socially, psychologically, and historically.

Finally, the dinosaur fossils themselves give no evidence or support for evolution. They appear to be remains of created creatures. The rocks in which they are found indicate that they were deposited by a catastrophic flood of great intensity and scope — just as described in the Bible.

Is There a Lost World?

There is no lost world of dangerous, dueling dinosaurs. There is no lost world of primeval forested swamps cooking up a soup of single-celled prototypes of later species. But there is a *lost world*. It is a lost world of humanity, teeming with individuals who daily struggle to find purpose in life, as they seek to understand the past. What is the best explanation for life's history?

If creation is true, and the evidence from both science and Scripture allude to that, then it has application for each one of us. If God is truly the Creator of all things, including man in His image, then, as stated earlier, He also has the authority to make the laws, and set the guidelines for life. Furthermore, He has the authority to set the penalty for breaking His laws. As created beings, our responsibility is obedience. God has said, "The wages of sin is death" (Rom. 6:23). Sin is disobedience to God's laws, and punishment for sin is death. Death is external separation from God and anything righteous, just, and holy. The Bible describes a place called hell, the "lake of fire" (Rev. 20:15), a place of eternal torment, of "weeping and gnashing of teeth" (Matt. 8:12) as the eternal destiny of those who reject God. Sinners shall be locked in sin, suffering its awful consequences forever.

The Bible says that "all have sinned, and come short of the glory of God" (Rom. 3:23). No one can deny sin (Rom. 3:10–11). Thus, man is unable to help himself and has no hope. Ah, but there is hope, there is one possible solution. If God himself, being sinless, were to become a Man and pay the penalty for us, then we would be free of sin's penalty. That is just what God did!

Jesus Christ, God the Son, himself the Creator, offended by the rejection of His creatures, the One who pronounced sin's awful penalty, loved His creation so much that He was willing to do what was necessary, to die to set us free. Romans 5:8 tells us, "But God commendeth His love toward us, in that, while we were yet sinners, Christ died for us." God, the Creator of life, was God the Son willing to die in our place and thus take our death penalty on himself. Since Jesus never sinned, He was the only One who could stop the succession of sin and death. Jesus Christ died for our sin and then He came back to life, rising from the grave in victory over sin and death, offering us forgiveness from sin, freedom from sin's bondage, and everlasting life. The Bible promises that "For God so loved the world, that He gave His only begotten Son, that whosoever believeth in Him should not perish, but have everlasting life" (John 3:16). "The wages of sin is death, but the gift of God is eternal life through Jesus Christ our Lord" (Rom. 6:23). "For whosoever shall call upon the name of the Lord shall be saved" (Rom. 10:13).

This is God's message to you of dinosaurs. First, they teach that God is the Almighty Creator, the King over all His creation, including you and me. Next, they remind us of the presence of sin in creation, the conscious choice of Adam and Eve and everyone since. Sin's penalty is death. It was in Adam's day, it was in Noah's day, and it still is today. Dinosaur fossils are dead things, and while animals don't sin, the penalty for Adam's sin affects all of creation. All things die under God's penalty, expressed scientifically as the second law of thermodynamics. Death is physical, but more serious for mankind, it is also spiritual. Christ, the Creator of dinosaurs and people, died to restore His creation to its original created intent. And He's coming back as King. This knowledge brings responsibility which must lead to a decision and action. Are you ready to do business with God?

All that God requires is that we acknowledge our own sinfulness and that we deserve sin's penalty. We must recognize that God the Son, Jesus Christ, died to pay that penalty for us. Each person must, in heart-felt prayer, accept God's free gift of forgiveness, and ask God to apply Christ's death to his own sin. Our loving and merciful God will respond with the gifts of forgiveness, eternal life with Him, and the power to live a life of victory over sin!

For whosoever shall call upon the name of the Lord shall be saved (Rom. 10:13).

Additional books on this topic:

Dinosaurs by Design
Dinosaurs of Eden
The Great Dinosaur Mystery Solved
Noah's Ark and the Ararat Adventure
What Really Happened to the Dinosaurs?

available from

Master Books
P.O. Box 727
Green Forest, AR 72638